The Garden of Earthly Delights

by
Adriana Picker

hardie grant books

Flowers bloom, lizards leap, bees swarm and mushrooms emerge in this earthy exploration of the natural world. Take your time to colour every intricately drawn petal, leaf, moth, worm and bug to help you centre yourself on firm ground.

Peer through the foliage to discover all strata of the garden landscape: from soaring birds and fluttering dragonflies, rustling leaves and towering blooms, right down to scattering bugs and wriggling worms.

Welcome to
The Garden of Earthly Delights!

Adriana Picker grew up around nature. Born in Gosford, Australia, she has lived in Newcastle, Sydney, the Blue Mountains and other places where plants and artists seem to thrive. At the heart of Adriana's work is a lifelong love of botanical illustration.

As an illustrator and designer, Adriana's work has spanned vast fields. Her costume illustrations have twice been shown at the Oscars; she has hand-drawn advertising for clients such as Absolut Vodka; and her work has appeared in a variety of books and magazines.

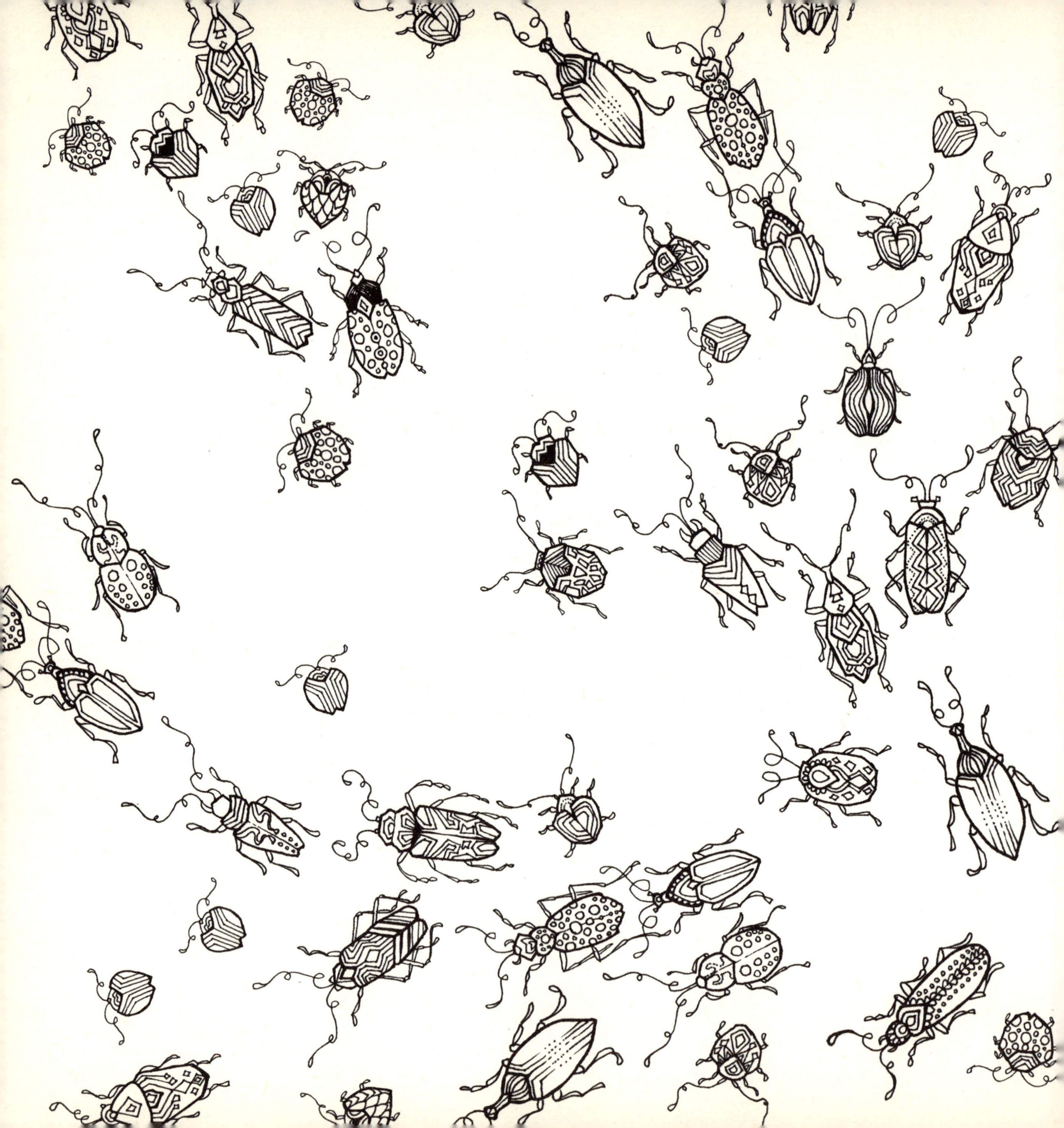

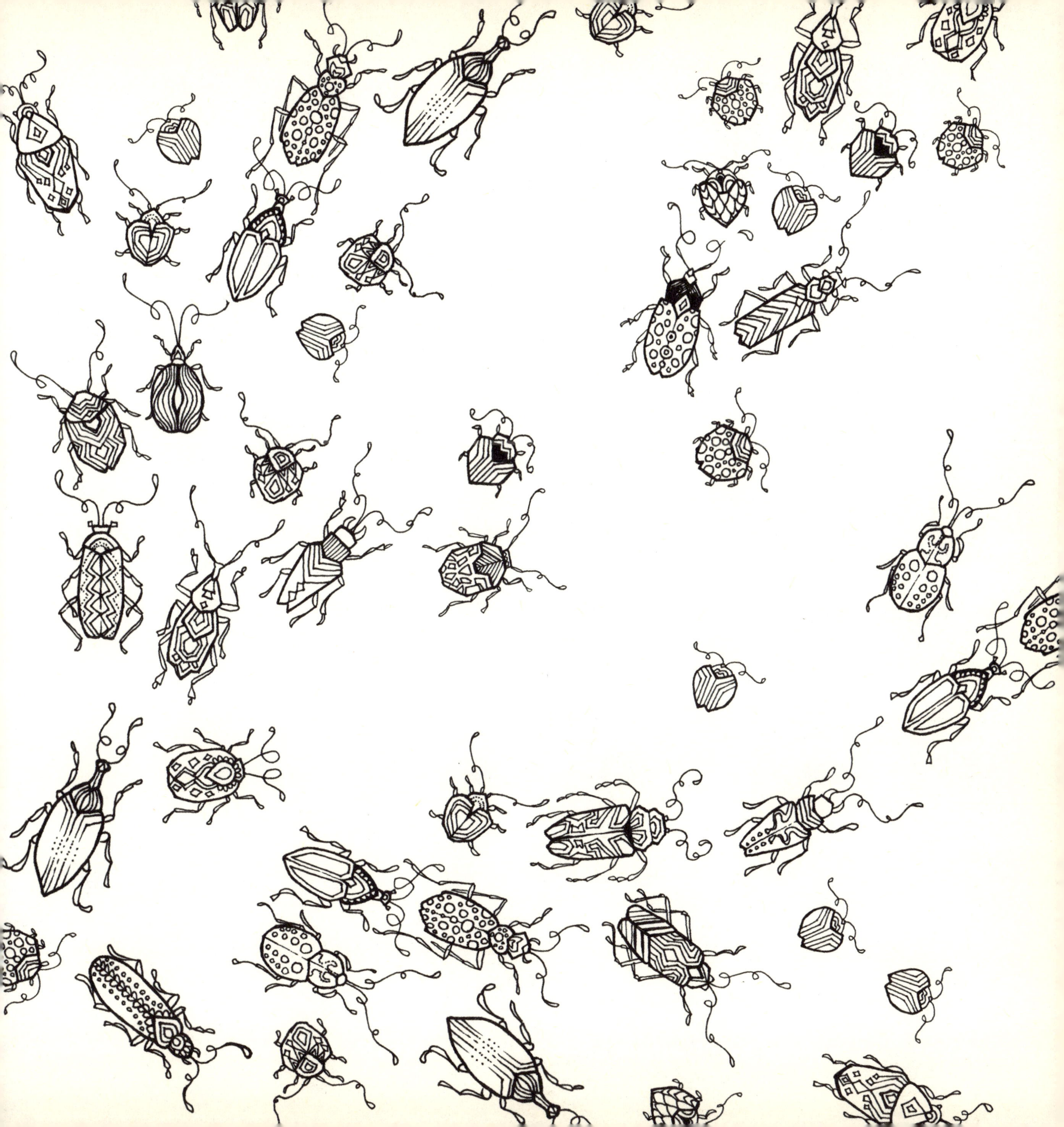

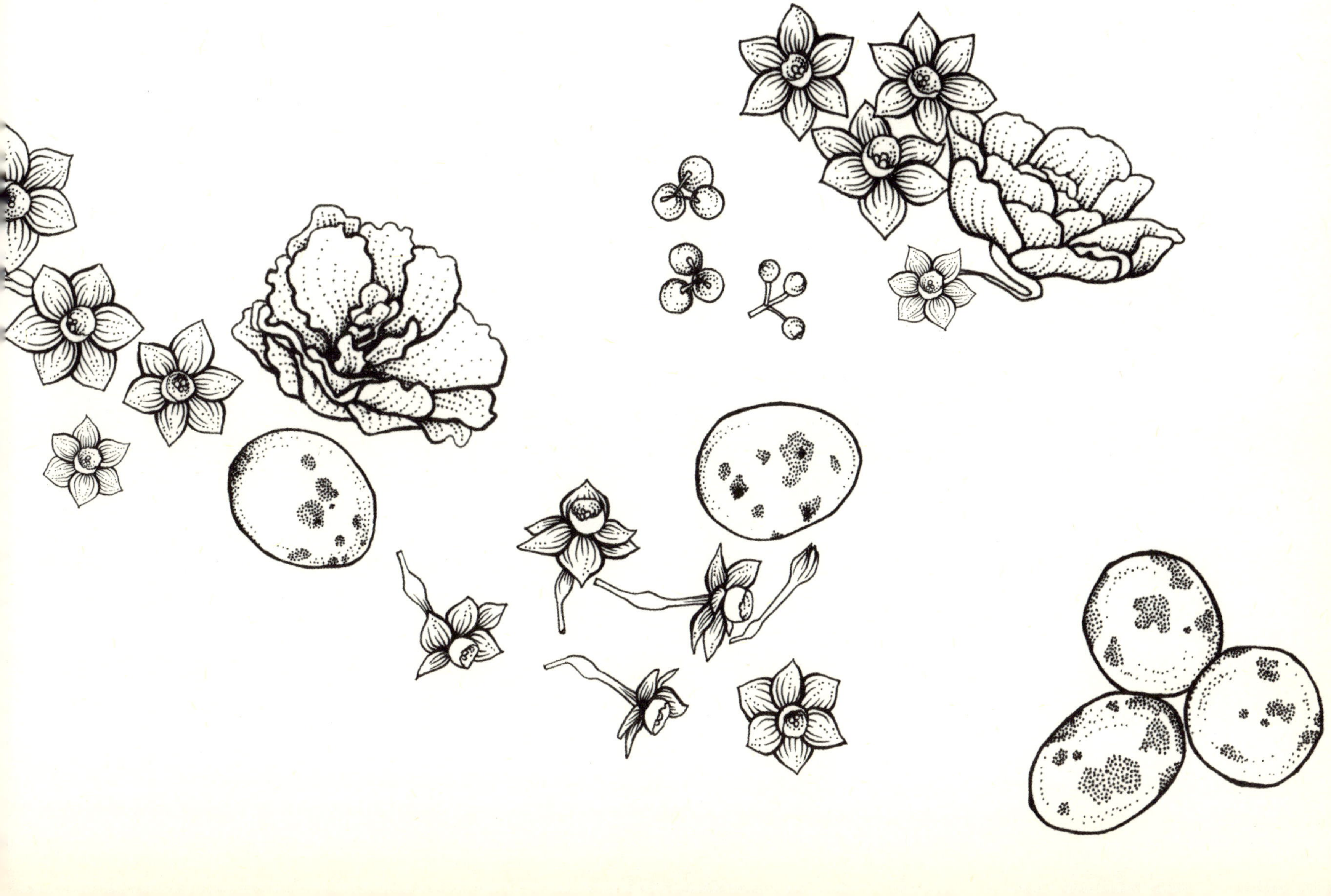

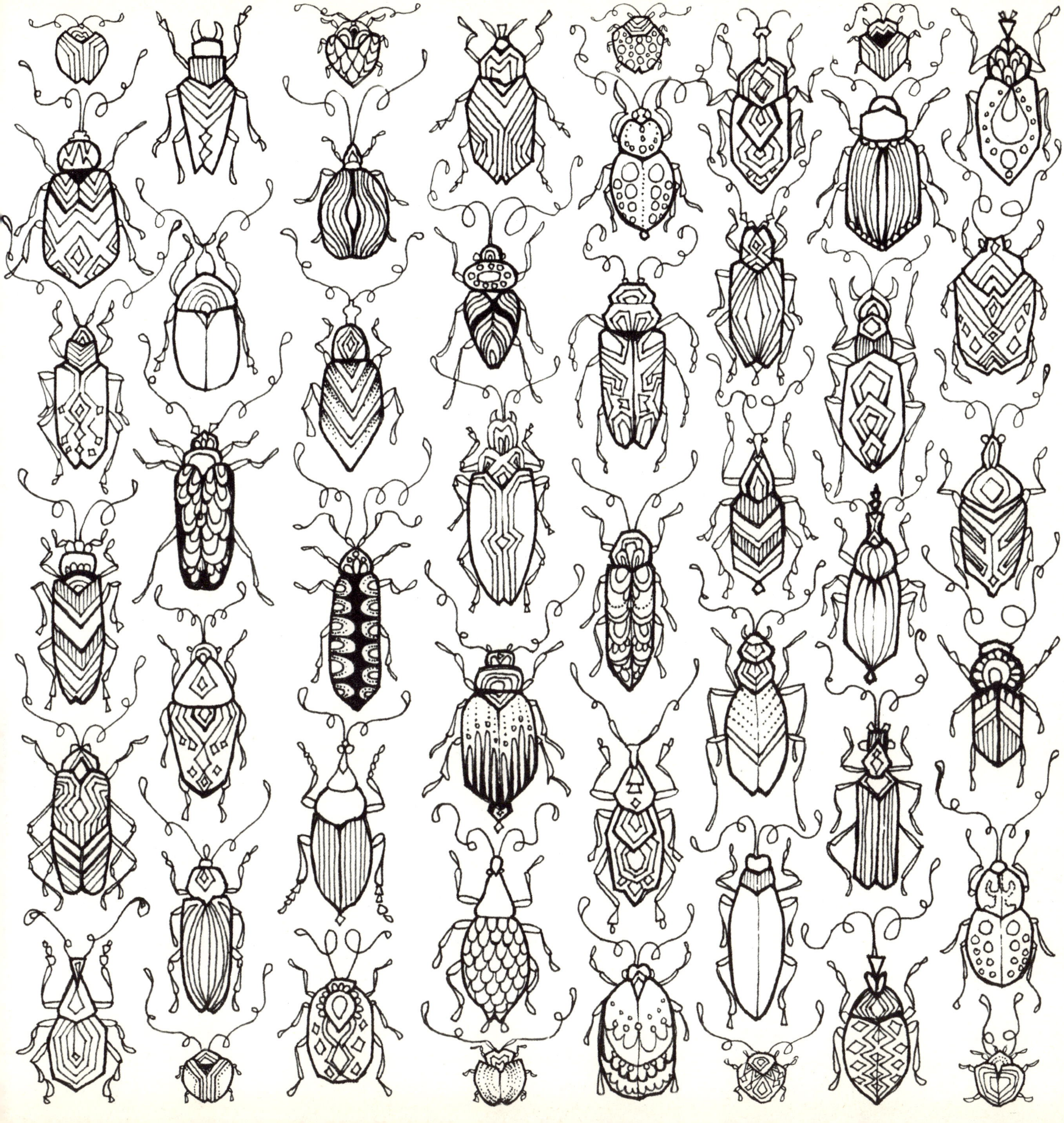

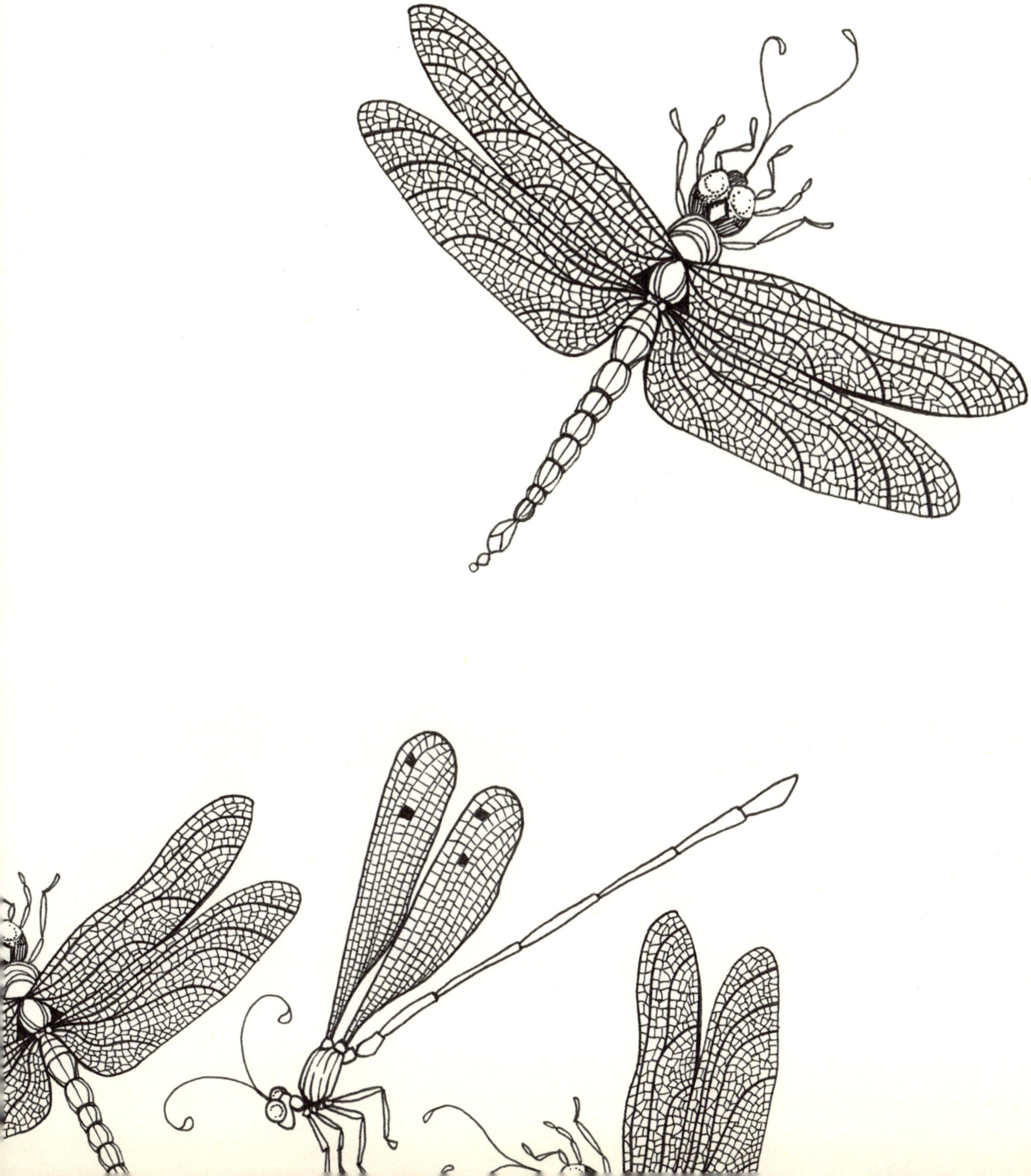

Published in 2015 by Hardie Grant Books

Hardie Grant Books (Australia)
Ground Floor, Building 1
658 Church Street
Richmond, Victoria 3121
www.hardiegrant.com.au

Hardie Grant Books (UK)
5th & 6th Floors
52-54 Southwark Street
London SE1 1UN
www.hardiegrant.co.uk

A Cataloguing-in-Publication entry is available from the catalogue of the National Library of Australia at www.nla.gov.au

The Garden of Earthly Delights
ISBN 978 1 74379 095 3
U.S. ISBN 978 1 74379 104 2

Publishing Director: Fran Berry
Project Editor: Rachel Day
Design Manager: Mark Campbell
Production Manager: Todd Rechner

Printed in China by 1010 Printing International Limited